GOSPEL DRAMAS

TWELVE PLAYS FOR WORSHIP IN LENT AND OTHER SEASONS

DEAN NADASDY

AUGSBURG Publishing House • Minneapolis

*These dramas are dedicated to
KRISTIN, MOLLY, and PHILIP,
who have already begun to see
the grace of the master Playwright
in the dramas of their lives.*

GOSPEL DRAMAS
Twelve Plays for Worship in Lent and Other Seasons

Copyright © 1985 Augsburg Publishing House

Scripture quotations unless otherwise noted are from the Revised Standard Version of the Bible, copyright 1946, 1952, and 1971 by the Division of Christian Education of the National Council of Churches.

The dramas "Six Shades of Purple" are reprinted with permission from *Resources for Youth Ministry*, 80.1, a quarterly publication of the Board for Youth Services of The Lutheran Church–Missouri Synod, 1333 S. Kirkwood Road, St. Louis, Missouri, 63122. Used by permission.

Library of Congress Cataloging-in-Publication Data

Nadasdy, Dean,1947–
  GOSPEL DRAMAS.

  Contents: Our church—"I tried to tell them"—
What about the plant?—Every party has a pooper—
[etc.]
  1. Christian drama, American. I. Title.
PS3564.A28G6   1985   812'.54   85-22886
ISBN 0-8066-2185-0

Manufactured in the U.S.A.   APH 10-2829

1   2   3   4   5   6   7   8   9   0   1   2   3   4   5   6   7   8   9

Contents

page 4   Acknowledgments
     5   Let There Be Drama in the Church

Six Shades of Purple
   12   Our Church
   19   "I Tried to Tell Them"
   25   "What about the Plant?"
   29   Every Party Has a Pooper
   33   "The Very Stone"
   38   "What Do You Mean, 'He's Here Already'?"

Dramas from an Upper Room
   44   "Jesus Saves"
   50   "Pardon Me, but Who Died?"
   58   The Sedentary Life
   65   In the Middle of "In-between"
   72   Losing It
   79   Six People, One Pew

   86   Were You There? (A Dramatic Worship Event for Good Friday)

Acknowledgments

Special thanks to Wanda Berke and Claire Oie, office staff of Cross View Lutheran Church, Edina, Minnesota, and good friends, who typed the manuscript for this book.

My gratitude to the members of Grace Lutheran Church, Eugene, Oregon, and Cross View Lutheran Church, Edina, Minnesota, who first took the roles in these dramas, presenting them in a worship setting. Their mood of adventure and spirit of celebration helped bring holy laughter to two seasons of Lent.

DEAN NADASDY

Let There Be Drama in the Church

Here's an interesting question. When was the last time you were surprised in a worship service? I asked a friend of mine that very question. He was a confirmed churchgoer, who had seen his share of worshiping communities.

After thinking for a moment, my friend's face lit up with his recollection of the last great surprise in worship. He told me about the preacher who came out on Sunday morning looking his usual prim and proper self. In the corner, near his chair in the chancel, was a small, circulating fan. The well-meaning custodian had placed the fan on the floor, anticipating a hot morning. The fan looked as if it had been around since the last century.

Anyway, as the pastor returned to his chair to sing a hymn, unaccustomed to the fan's presence, he caught the edge of his fine, white alb in the fan's blades. The fan ripped into that alb, my friend told me, like a hungry animal as the congregation watched its pastor fight and finally win in the struggle to keep his robe.

Word has it that the congregation never saw that fan again. The pastor wasn't hurt, but he surely had the undivided attention of his audience.

This recollection wasn't exactly what I had in mind when I asked about a surprise in church, but it well illustrates the point that most drama in worship is neither planned nor rehearsed. It just happens, and, as a matter of fact, we love it and remember it.

The church is asking for drama. Its yawns and clichés signal its hunger for surprise. The gospel asks for drama. God's own dramatic flare is written across the gospel's script of unseen turns, vivid characters, and crucibles of conflict.

When the Word became flesh, drama became the property of the church. We'll always ask for drama as long as the gospel is as real to us as life itself. What's more, many of us are convinced that the gospel itself holds more surprise than a pastor on Sunday doing chancel warfare with a fan.

Drama in Worship

Using drama in worship brings some welcome ingredients to a service recipe. When you perform a little drama in front of your worshiping fellowship, they are blessed with the following experiences:

1. *Identification.* Worshipers see characters with whom they can identify. As the characters struggle and grow, worshipers struggle and grow with them.

2. *Surprise.* The unexpected twist in a plot or the surprise on the face of a player brings freshness and serendipity to the worship experience.

3. *Rootedness.* Drama presents life. As such, it sets the gospel in the context of real living. Drama is the Word with skin on it.

4. *Tension and Conflict.* Drama at its best presents a struggle. Tension is central to the Christian experience. Drama pictures the conflicts of law/gospel, sinner/saint, good/evil, now/not yet, and many more.

5. *Participation.* Drama puts more people up front in worship and invites people to feel, to think, and to respond.

6. *Coherence.* A drama in worship provides one more medium for expressing the service's central theme, often struck by the Gospel for the Day.

7. *A Foil.* Drama as foil is an important aspect of drama used in worship. Most of the dramas in this book are designed as foils for the gospel. Through drama, worshipers can be "set up" to hear the gospel proclaimed. Drama as a foil prepares people for good news. More than that, it moves people to want the gospel after witnessing what life without it is like.

The Dramas in This Book

This book contains two series of dramas designed to be used in worship services. Each series includes six dramas, each based on a gospel reading. Though the dramas are based on Lenten texts, they may be presented in other seasons of the church year as well.

The dramas are intentionally short, each requiring about two hours of rehearsal time. Few actors are needed. The set furnishings and props are minimal.

Each drama contains a "Focus" section, signaling the message of the drama as drawn from the

Bible text; a "Characters" section, suggesting some character traits for the players; and a "Setting" section with helps on staging.

The first series, "Six Shades of Purple," is based on the gospels from Luke for the six Sundays in Lent (Series C). Because these dramas may be used in a liturgical service, their placing is significant. For the most part, the dramas are meant to be presented after the gospel is read and before the sermon is preached. A hymn may separate the drama and the sermon. The dramas should serve the preacher well in preparing people to hear the gospel. Further, the dramas provide ready-made characters and events for illustration, parable, and application.

The second series, "Dramas from an Upper Room," is based on the Upper Room Discourses of Jesus in John 13-17. As with the first series, the dramas serve best as primers for preaching. Each grows out of a thought expressed by Christ as he spoke and prayed with his disciples. The dramas are designed to be presented in a Lenten midweek worship setting.

Following each of the dramas are "Primers for Preaching," helps for preachers as they seek to put the drama to work in the pulpit. Also provided are "Discussion Starters," since the dramas may be used in a setting where worshipers can converse about the drama's themes.

A worship design for Good Friday, "Were You There," is also provided. The chancel drama in the service brings forth voices from the passion narrative as worshipers hear the seven last words of Christ from the cross. The sounding of bell tones denotes the passing of time and the completion of his atoning work. The spiritual, "Were You There?" provides the mood for the drama. The traditional solemn recessional concludes the event with the singing of "Now the Light Has Gone Away."

Some Don'ts

1. Don't ask for volunteers to be in the dramas. Recruit a troupe of talented players who will commit themselves to presenting several of the dramas in the Lenten season. You may have the makings of an ongoing drama troupe!

2. Don't bite off more than you can chew. If doing all six dramas in a series is impossible, choose fewer and do them well.

3. Don't limit your players to a single age group. Drama presents a fine opportunity for intergenerational ministry. The dramas in this book are intentionally designed to include all age groups.

4. Don't wait until the last minute for recruitment and rehearsal. Just as the church choir needs time to rehearse, a drama troupe must be given time, too. Remember, two hours of rehearsal per drama is about right.

5. Don't let the dramas stand by themselves. You may wish to print the "Focus" section in the worship folder so that people know the central point of the drama. Again, these dramas are meant to be followed up with gospel preaching and/or discussion.

Some Dos

1. Do integrate the dramas into the flow and message of the entire worship design. Strive for coherence.

2. Do work on developing a character if you're a player in a drama. Don't settle for memorizing lines. Be someone real.

3. Do be ready for some laughter, even if it is Lent. The church always has a reason to smile and to laugh.

4. Do see preparing these dramas as an opportunity for sharing in community and for ministry.

5. Do expect to do more drama. It's catching.

Six Shades of Purple

*Six Dramas Based on the Gospels
for the Six Sundays in Lent
(Series C)*

Our Church

A Chancel Drama for Lent 1 (Series C)

Bible Text:

Luke 4:1-13

Focus:

People in church are not always what they seem. They have their wildernesses where they struggle with sin, death, and the devil. Still, they are a victorious people in Christ.

Characters:

USHER—inviting; homespun; has depth and compassion

BUCK—16 years old; searching for an answer

FRIEDA—in her 70s; full of self-pity

MAX—business-type; appears more sure of himself than he is

SARAH—uneasy; looking for a way out

PASTOR—robed and in place

Setting:

Your church in its regular morning worship service.

(As the scene opens, the USHER *who has served as an usher as people arrived now "steps into" the service in the style of the Stage Manager in Thornton Wilder's* Our Town. *Characters sit on chairs staggered about the front of the church. Their hymnals are open. The pastor sits in his normal place. A spotlight [overhead projectors work well here] that moves from person to person would enhance the action.)*

USHER: *(Enters up center aisle as the singing of a hymn concludes.)* Real fine, folks. We're sounding better and better. Don't know how long you've been here, but was the time when the organ out-sounded the singing around here. Singing has a way of outdoing just about everything if you think about it. Why, hearing you sing, you'd think the world was gilded royal, and you and I aren't much different from the angels! Well, I suppose we have our better moments, you and I, when we climb the heights and keep company with archangels; but underneath the hallelujahs, deep under the saintly smiles we see around here, are struggles never seen but by the soul that bears them. *(Has lapsed off; gathers himself.)* Don't mean to depress you this morning. But come along. I'll show you what I mean. (*Spot to* BUCK; USHER *walks over to stand behind* BUCK *who remains frozen with hymnal open.)* Buck here is 16. Plays football fairly well, enough to play every game over at the high school last fall. You can tell when Buck walks into church on Sunday.

Every young gal's head turns—one or two, by
the way, more than others. He's a popular boy,
Buck is. Truth is people tend to put him on a
pedestal. The All-American Boy. Most of you
know that Buck's dad passed away last year.
What you don't know is what goes on inside of
Buck even all these months later. His mother
knows, though. She's heard it, how hard it is
for Buck to understand. Listen.

BUCK: (*Comes to life; stands as if talking to mother.*) I don't get it, mom. Dad gives all he's got
for the church, and then God lets him die. It
isn't fair. We prayed, all of us. It just seems like
there ought to be some kind of payoff for a guy
like dad. (*Pauses.*) Oh, I know, there's heaven.
But he never saw me grow up all the way. I never
told him how much I loved him. Mom, why
didn't God do something? Didn't he know how
much I would miss dad? (*Returns to chair;
opens hymnal; into frozen position; spot from
BUCK to FRIEDA.*)

FRIEDA: (*Begins rocking in her rocking chair and
speaks with obvious self-pity.*) Sometimes
being dead is better than being alive. I'm not
doing much good for anybody here. Might win
a rock-a-thon, I guess. (*Chuckles audibly; sar-
castically.*) And now our winner, Frieda Schul-
mann, who has rocked in this same chair day
in and day out for the last 10 years! Let's hear
it for Frieda, folks! . . . Silence. Does anybody
know that Frieda's here? Is anybody listening?
(*USHER moves beside her; FRIEDA freezes with
hymnal open; no longer rocks.*)

USHER: We're listening, Frieda. (*To audience.*)
Get my meaning, folks? The struggle 'neath the

hallelujahs. Crossbearing, some might call it.
The temptation to give it up for an easier way.
(*Walks over to* MAX; *spot from* FRIEDA *to* MAX.)
You know, I've heard it said that for every
mountain there's a valley. Take Max here. Most
of you know Max as a leader of our church. Why,
I don't know if there's a position in this congregation that Max hasn't held. Last Friday,
Max squeaked a deal through at work that was
a little shady (*pauses to catch audience's reaction*). Oh, I know, not Max! And Max himself
can't believe it. He's doing what you might call
fudging . . . on God . . . on himself. It isn't easy
to face God or yourself when you've given in to
temptation. Max's argument runs something
like this.

MAX: (*Stands in front of mirror placed near his
chair.*) Max Robinson, you're not all you think
you are. You knew right well that property
would depreciate in value within 10 years. Why
didn't you tell him that?. . . He should have
known it, though. You don't buy property without checking it out thoroughly. The responsi-
bility was his, not mine. . . . I'll never see the
guy again anyway. I think he kind of liked me.
. . . Well, I'll make up for it on the next deal. . . .
Hope it works out for him, though. (*Returns to
chair; opens hymnal; freezes; spot from* MAX
to SARAH.)

SARAH: (*Stands and speaks as if to her hus-
band.*) Bill, I don't know if I can go on. I need
room to breathe. I'm tired of it all, the kids, the
house, the stores, the wash. Can't we just say
it's been a good 10 years and leave each other
alone. All we do is fight (*pauses as if for response*). No! If we can't settle it ourselves, I'm

sure not going to see some counselor! You can do better than me anyway. Bill, I just have to start over again. It isn't working the way I had thought it would. (*Returns to chair; opens hymnal.* USHER *walks to stand beside her.*)

USHER: So the struggle, from one soul to the next. And you can drape a soul in long white robes and christen it a "Reverend," (*walks over to* PASTOR; *spot to* PASTOR) but still the tempting and the cross are there. The pastor climbs into his pulpit to give his weekly dosage of the Word to heal the ills of humankind. (PASTOR *moves to pulpit and opens Bible.*) But in that one brief moment before he reads his text and speaks with some authority, he wonders with words that for once we can hear. . . .

PASTOR: I wonder if they'll listen today. . . . There's Louise. She'll listen. She's always waiting for me to slip up on something . . . . And Frank there . . . . You want a pillow, Frank? . . . Do any of them know what I paid for this sermon, the hours away from Sue and the kids? . . . I've got to talk to Sue about the time away from home. I know it's getting to her . . . . Well, here goes, Lord. Forgive the lazy preparation! Forgive the shortcuts! . . . Oh, why apologize? I'm three steps above the preacher up the street . . . Sue? Are you going to listen today? Are you? . . . (*Smiles a pastoral smile.*) Grace, mercy, and peace to you . . . . (*Freezes at pulpit; spot to* USHER *center-stage;* PASTOR *returns to chair.*)

USHER: So there it is, our church, or some small sample of the struggles we have with sin, and death, and the devil. (*Chuckles.*) Even preachers know about such things! We all have our stories, every one. Yet we are all here Sunday by Sunday, singing to be heard. We whisper in the wind of the Spirit that somehow again this Sunday we will hear some word, say some prayer, touch some miracle that will help us sing again come next Lord's Day. That is the saving grace of all of this, that we are together here in hope, that we can believe once more that for every valley there is a mountain. Sure. This is how it is. "This is the way we are: in our growing up and in our marrying and in our living and in our dying."* (*The congregation sings "Blest Be the Tie That Binds," as spot moves from character to character.*)

Primers for Preaching

1. Christians struggle every day with the temptation to evade the cross for easier paths to glory.

2. Appearances can be deceiving. People in church may look trouble-free while underneath they struggle to understand and to overcome.

3. Jesus' temptation recorded in Luke 4:1-13 was a temptation to forsake the passion for immediate glory. The easier way is not always the right way.

4. Despite our personal struggles and crosses, we are still together as a church. We gather because the gospel always holds hope before us.

5. The church must seek ways to support those who fight their secret battles with sin, death, and the devil.

---

*Thornton Wilder, *Our Town* (New York: Harper & Row, 1938).

Discussion Starters

1. James 1:13-15 offers some basic principles regarding temptation. According to these verses, to whom does temptation come? Does God ever send temptation? Is temptation primarily an individual or a corporate experience? How does temptation work? Try and find answers to these questions in these verses.

2. In what way(s) is your life more difficult because you are a Christian?

3. What can the church do to support those who face ongoing struggles and doubts?

4. With whom can you be completely honest, shaking off the mask of "all is well," even when it isn't? Who are your encouragers?

"I Tried to Tell Them"

A Chancel Drama for Lent 2 (Series C)

Bible Text:

Luke 13:31-35

Focus:

Jesus loved Jerusalem and its people with a tender, compassionate heart. He looked on its failures with warm, loving kindness. Jesus still deals compassionately with us and offers dreams of something better.

Characters:

OLD MAN—warm and fatherly; touched by what he sees

GIRL—about 10 years old; engrossed by her aging visitor

Setting:

An inner-city blighted area.

(*As the scene opens,* GIRL *is skipping rope.*)

OLD MAN: (*Silently enters and stands watching girl skip rope.*)

GIRL: (*After awhile she notices she is being watched and doesn't like it.*) Take a picture, Mister. It lasts longer!

OLD MAN: No thanks, I have a picture.

GIRL: (*Still skipping rope.*) Of me? Really? You've got a picture of me?

OLD MAN: Of you and many others who have skipped rope here before you.

GIRL: Really into rope-skipping, huh? Or is it rope-skippers you like? Maybe I shouldn't be talking to you.

OLD MAN: As you like it.

GIRL: (*Skips rope; silence;* OLD MAN *continues watching her; she finally stops.*) You want to show me your picture, don't you?

OLD MAN: I can't.

GIRL: Why not?

OLD MAN: (*Pointing to his own head.*) They're up here . . . (*pointing to his own heart*) and in here.

GIRL: (*Dubiously.*) Oh. (*Silence; fills silence by taking jump rope and making a circle out of it on the ground.*)

OLD MAN: A circle marks the spot.

GIRL: What spot, Mister?

OLD MAN: Where you and I and many others have stood, and jumped and dreamt before.

GIRL: Do I know you, Mister?

OLD MAN: No. But I know this place. It's sort of a holy place for me.

GIRL: Mister, I know this place, and there ain't nothing holy about it.

OLD MAN: That's because you don't see it the way I do. (*Extending hand to* GIRL.) Come on, I'll show you.

GIRL: Nothing doin'.

OLD MAN: Will you at least walk behind me?. . . Trust me.

GIRL: (*Picks up rope and follows him stage right.*) Where are we going?

OLD MAN: There. That building. What do you see?

GIRL: Nothing up there except Old Lady Finnegan. Cops call her a squatter. Buzz says he thinks that building will be the next to burn. What do you see, Mister?

OLD MAN: I see the Finnegans, the McCalls, the Daytons, and the Cunninghams. Good strong, happy families living in that four family flat, cutting out a piece of life and a place they once called home.

GIRL: Oh, yeah?

OLD MAN: (*Leads her to stage right.*) And there, (*pointing*) what do you see there?

GIRL: A parking lot that ain't used much for anything except dumpin' junk.

OLD MAN: I see old Saint Andrew's, a parish of 1200 strong. Those old church bells used to ring every Sunday morning at 7:30; and if you weren't up then, you got up, 'cause the singing would keep you awake anyway.

GIRL: Not much singin' coming from that parking lot.

OLD MAN: (*Caught by the vision of times past.*) And there (*points center-backstage*), what's right there?

GIRL: Nothin', Mister, the liquor store moved out of there last month. It's just empty now.

OLD MAN: Then it was "Stosh's Ice Cream Parlor," the best on the near South Side.

GIRL: Then? What do you mean, "then"?

OLD MAN: When I was your age on this street.

GIRL: I never thought about how it used to look. I guess I thought it always looked like this.

OLD MAN: I tried to tell them.

GIRL: Tell them what?

OLD MAN: That if they moved away, and sold it all, and left the neighborhood behind, it would turn out like this.

GIRL: Well, is this so bad, Mister? This is my home you're talking about, you know.

OLD MAN: And my home, too. It's only bad when you see it with these eyes, little girl. How often I've wanted to bring it all back, the families, the church bells, the sounds of people laughing, and the hope in people's eyes, the look of progress on the face of every building, but it can be no more. There is only us two, and your eyes are too young to see as I see.

GIRL: Aw, come on. (OLD MAN *begins to exit weeping in his handkerchief.*) It ain't that bad. You wanna watch me jump rope some more? (OLD MAN *has exited.*) Mister? Mister? (*She returns to jumping rope.*)

Primers for Preaching

1. Jesus sees us not only as we are but also as we've been and as we still can be.

2. Despite our failures, Jesus is compassionate toward us.

3. It cuts to the heart to see what one loves erode and decay. Jesus had that experience in Luke 13:31-35.

4. In a world of constant change there is Jesus with constant compassion.

5. What do you see when you look at a center-city area today? Hopeless blight or an opportunity to serve?

Discussion Starters

1. What message did the old man try to convey to the girl?

2. How was the old man like Jesus in Luke 13:31-35? How was he different?

3. When have you "mourned" the changes you've seen in a place or in a person dear to you?

4. In the midst of a neighborhood's decay, there was this old man who had been there through it all. He was a constant with change all around. Where do you find constancy today? What contribution does Christianity make to your security in a changing world?

5. The little girl never understood what the old man was trying to tell her. What were her limitations? Why couldn't she understand?

6. What pictures today in the news media cut through to your heart and ask for compassion and active love?

"What about the Plant?"

A Chancel Drama for Lent 3 (Series C)

Bible Text:
Luke 13:1-9

Focus:
God is patient with us. He doesn't discard us for our shortcomings, but nurtures us to spiritual wholeness.

Characters:

SCOTT—anxious to get out of the old house; hurried; pushing
LINDA—willing to take time for "a friend"

Setting:
An empty room except for one large box and a large drooping plant that looks near death.

(As scene opens, LINDA is packing things in the large carton.)

LINDA: (*Packs up and closes carton;* SCOTT *enters stage left.*)·That's it, Scott. The last one! I thought we'd never see the day!

SCOTT: (*Looks around.*) Aren't you forgetting something? (*Points to sick plant.*) Shall I just set it out with the garbage or what?

LINDA: No, don't do that!

SCOTT: (*Facetiously.*) Well, how about sending it to Aunt Gertrude? (*Lifts drooping branches on plant and then lets them drop.*) A suitable gift, wouldn't you say?

LINDA: Scott!

SCOTT: (*Getting impatient; wants to move on.*) I'll carry this last box out, and while I'm outside, you say your good-byes to "Old Limpy" here. (*Lifts box and exits.*)

LINDA: (*Checks to be sure that she is completely alone; then stoops down to address plant.*) You and I have been through a lot together, you know. We came to this place together. I watched you grow. I tried my best to keep you healthy. I even started my one-way conversations with you when Susie said it worked for their weeping fig . . . although after all her talk her weeping fig is still weeping. But you have no excuse. Now I have to decide what to do with you.

SCOTT: (*Breathless.*) What's it gonna be, Linda? It doesn't look any better than when I left. Tell you what. Here's some advice. Keep the pot and dump the plant. It's an embarrassment anyway. After all those horticulture classes, I had hoped to see the greening of your thumb. But look at it. (*Points to plant.*) Tell me that's going to add to the decor of our new home.

LINDA: OK, Scott, take it. Set it out with the garbage. I tried, but it just won't come back. Go ahead. (SCOTT *lifts pot and starts to exit stage left.*) Scott!

SCOTT: (*Stops dead in his tracks.*) What now?

LINDA: I've changed my mind.

SCOTT: To Aunt Gertrude with love?

LINDA: No. I want to give it more time.

SCOTT: How much time?

LINDA: As long as it takes.

SCOTT: Too long. I don't want that sad excuse for a living thing looking at me every day for the next 10 years. Did it ever occur to you that the thing might be used to being sick and likes it?

LINDA: Give me six months, Scott, to nurse it back to health.

SCOTT: And then? What happens if it doesn't get any better?

LINDA: Then it's the garbage can. OK?

SCOTT: (*Both begin to exit.*) We make a good team, we three: (*points to Linda*) the good, (*points to himself*) the bad, (*points to the plant*) and the ugly. (*To plant.*) I'll never know what she sees in you, buddy, but you have a new home and another chance.

LINDA: Be careful with it, Scott. (*Exit stage left.*)

Primers for Preaching

1. The Lord is certainly more patient with us than we are with others.

2. When we fail, the Lord doesn't discard us but nurtures us back to spiritual wholeness.

3. Better than criticism and judgment is a spirit of patient nurture. How different would the people around us be if we saw their potential instead of their flaws?

4. Salvation is not a contingency-free exchange. There is a time contingency (Luke 13:8-9). We have only a lifetime in which to bear fruit.

5. Where genuine Christ-like love characterizes a relationship, there will be an investment of time and encouragement.

Discussion Starters

1. Talk about a time when it seemed as if everyone had given up on you, except one or two who stood by you. Who were your steadfast supporters?

2. As Linda spoke with her plant, what similarities did you notice between Linda and our Lord as he relates to us?

3. What good news do the parable of the fig tree and this little drama hold for Christian parents whose grown children have separated themselves from the church?

4. Scott was too busy to be concerned with the plant. What made Linda give the plant time and concern? Why do we sometimes "discard" others? What makes us give up on them?

5. Who are society's disposable people today, asking for ministry from God's people?

Every Party Has a Pooper

A Chancel Drama for Lent 4 (Series C)

Bible Text:

Luke 15:1-3, 11-32

Focus:

Some people miss the fact that God welcomes sinners home with open arms. They may see the Lord only as a judge.

Characters:

E.S.—"E.S." Stands for Elder Son; proud; confident; uncompromising

JOSH—a friend of E.S. who knows the father better than E.S.; fun-loving

Setting:

Simple setting. A prop to represent a tree or stack of straw is needed.

(*As the scene opens,* JOSH *and* E.S. *are sitting under the tree "shooting the breeze."*)

JOSH: Haven't seen much of your little brother, E.S. What's he up to?

E.S.:   No good, I'm sure. The guy's a loser.

JOSH: Where are you hiding him away?

E.S.:   You mean you haven't heard? The guy took off, took his inheritance and ran off.

JOSH: With the blond he was seeing in town?

E.S.:   Nope. Alone.

JOSH: He always was a restless one.

E.S.:   Stupid, too. I'd rather keep my money in the bank earning interest, what with inflation and all. You can't buy anything cheap anymore. The kid has to learn some patience. After all, dad isn't going to be around forever.

JOSH: You're a crass man, E.S.

E.S.:   Just honest Josh—and practical. The old man's not looking too good these days. He mopes around as if there were nothing to live for.

JOSH: He probably misses your little brother.

E.S.:   Maybe.

JOSH: Why don't we head out and look for the guy and surprise your dad? Wouldn't that be something! The look on his face when he sees us coming down the road together, all three of us!

E.S.:   Forget it, Josh. When Dad sees him, he is not going to be smiling. The kid's a drop-out, a lush! He's an embarrassment to the whole family. Dad won't even give him the time of day!

JOSH: You're awfully sure of yourself.

E.S.: I am the eldest son around here, you know, the only son right now. For all we know, my brother is dead by now. Anyway, he chose his road. Let him walk it alone. The guy's a loser.

JOSH: I still say, if he ever does come back . . . .

E.S.: The old man will have his hide! End of story. Meanwhile, it sure is nice being a one-and-only. (*Proudly settles back.*) Josh, I have it made. Dad demands little of me, but to keep him happy, I do just as he says, and I can't help but think that it will pay off in the end. If only little brother could see me now! (*Rises to exit.*) Josh, I'd like to while away the afternoon with you, but we gentlemen farmers do have chores to do, you know, to humor the man at the top. Stop by when you get a chance. (*Struts an exit.*)

JOSH: (*To audience.*) "Now his elder son was in the field; and as he came and drew near to the house, he heard music and dancing. And he called one of the servants and asked what it meant. And he said to him, 'Your brother has come, and your father has killed the fatted calf, because he has received him safe and sound.' "

Primers for Preaching

1. Though we may write people off as losers, our Lord welcomes losers into his family.

2. Like Pharisees, some Christians rest on their laurels, unwilling to give themselves to seeking the lost.

3. As hard as the Lord tries to teach us otherwise, some of us are content to see him only as a judge. We have yet to meet the Lord who throws parties for sinners!

4. Who is your little brother on the run? What can you do to bring him home?

Discussion Starters

1. Read Zephaniah 3:14-20. Note especially verses 17-18. The picture is one of God rejoicing over wayward Israel and bringing her home. It's God hosting a homecoming celebration! Why is it difficult for people to believe that God rejoices over his people "as on a day of a festival?"

2. E.S. in the drama did what he did on the farm "to humor the man at the top." He was a gentleman farmer with clean hands, no doubt. How much is expected of Christians by our Lord? Is being a Christian today easy or is it a dirty-hands enterprise?

3. Who in your life brings a party atmosphere to the Christian experience? Who makes life in Christ a celebration for you?

4. What can be done to encourage a church's commitment to go after its runaway sons and daughters? What are the obstacles for such a ministry? How are the obstacles overcome?

"The Very Stone"

A Chancel Drama for Lent 5 (Series C)

Bible Text:
Luke 20:9-19

Focus:
Though some reject the cornerstone that is Jesus Christ, others find it and there banquet on the grace of God.

Characters:

BARKER—estate auctioneer; high-brow but with a smidgen of down-home auctioneering still left in him; well-dressed

CROWD—a mixed bunch, some sophisticated, some rude, others noncommittal; have at least eight people in the crowd; four of these have speaking parts

COMIC FIGURE (C.F.)—dressed as mime with white face, suspenders, and tight-fitting shirt; moves in clownish fashion; carries look of delight over newly-found treasure

Setting:

A large estate where an auction is taking place. A visible stone made of paper mache and chicken wire and painted appropriately is the last item to be sold. The stone should have a reasonably flat surface on the top to serve as a table for C.F. Putting a spotlight on C.F. once the crowd exits would enhance the action.

(*As the scene opens, the last item, a large stone, is auctioned off. A crowd is gathered around auctioneer.*)

BARKER: And that, friends, leaves us with this, the very stone so dear to the departed for so many years. Surely one would expect the bidding to start at an honorable figure.

1:   (*Shouted out in heckler style.*) Sorry, pal, the pet rock craze has been over for a long time.

BARKER: Sir, this is no pet rock. It was the very stone on which the old mansion was built. A cornerstone, you might say. Yes, who will bid on this cornerstone, marked for all time as that which held together the Rutledge Mansion, the historic home of our most esteemed family?

2:   That's debatable, Barker. Old Man Rutledge was a slaver every day of his life. He treated people like pawns. Built his whole life on the work of others.

BARKER: (*Chooses to ignore comment.*) Do I have an opening bid?

3:   Five dollars!

BARKER: I didn't hear that, Billy Bob! We don't take bids of five dollars on any of our merchandise.

3:   I wouldn't exactly call that rock a piece of merchandise. I was just trying to take it off your hands. Why, it'll cost me that much to lug it over to the creek so the kids can jump off it into the water.

BARKER: I told you once, and I'll not repeat it, Billy Bob. We don't take bids of five dollars on anything.

2:   Why don't you buy the stone if you like it so much, Barker?

BARKER: I am seller here, ma'am, not buyer. Now, do we have an honorable bid or not?

1:   The man's worried. I can see it on his face. The guy's business is on the rocks, folks! (*Crowd laughs.*)

4:   (*With a sophisticated flair; steps before the crowd to* BARKER'S *rescue.*) Friends, perhaps we owe this stone and this good man a bit more respect than we seem willing to afford either of them. For if this stone is indeed the very cornerstone of the old mansion, it does possess some historic value. Might we not consider a bid befitting its value and propose a hallowed site for the stone in the town square, as a remembrance of the Golden Age of the South?

1:   Sounds good! (*To 4.*) Make your bid, Mr. Canning.

4:   I was suggesting, sir, a mutual bid from the members of the community gathered here. Could we not caucus and come to Mr. Barker with a bonafide offer on behalf of the town?

2: You're talking bond issue, Canning. The town won't even vote in the money for a stoplight. What makes you think they'd buy a rock?

BARKER: Do we have a bid? (*Silence.*)

3: What happens if you don't get a bid, Barker?

BARKER: My instructions are to leave the stone here.

3: Here? What good will it do anybody here?

BARKER: Those are my instructions. (*Glances at watch.*) Now for the last time, I ask for a bid on the stone. (*Silence.*) Thank you, ladies and gentlemen. This closes the estate auction. Kindly see the cashier at the gate as you leave. All items cash and carry. (BARKER *exits; crowd exits as they discuss the sale; the stone is left behind; stage/chancel lights down; spot to stone.*)

C.F.   (*Enters carrying sack over his shoulder; initially passes by stone; then looks back; smiles; returns to stone; walks around it, struggles to lift it; fails; looks to audience; smiles a broad smile; walks about stone again; sits on floor; leans against stone; naps for a count of 30; wakes; stands; looks in sack; removes tablecloth and places on top of rock; looks into sack again; removes loaf of bread and plate from sack and places these on tablecloth; looks into sack again; removes bottle of wine and glass and places them on tablecloth; stands before the meal; breaks bread; pours wine; reaches for bread; remembers; folds hands and raises head for prayer; smiles to audience; eats of bread; drinks of wine;*

smiles again, begins to pack bread away;
changes mind; puts all back in place; with
sweeping motion of his hands, makes invi-
tation for all to come; walks about stone with
broad smile; takes empty sack and exits as
spot highlights feast awaiting all.)

Primers for Preaching

1. People reject Christ as the cornerstone of their lives for many reasons. Instead of Christ, they build lives on the pursuit of fame, fortune, pleasure, and power. In the end, they may claim happiness; but a deeper, more abiding joy can be found in Christ, who comes to us with a banquet of forgiveness.

2. Christ is in the world. His presence is made known to us in word and in sacrament. The most important question faced by us is this: What shall I do with Jesus Christ?

3. Beware, lest we who "sell" the cornerstone fail to buy a piece of it ourselves.

4. So much talk—so little celebration. Take time for communing with Christ lest he be left behind in the dust of the church's business.

Discussion Starters

1. One man's garbage is another's treasure. Think of experiences in your life where this proverb has proved true.

2. People today may not openly reject Christ. More likely, they will ignore him. If you had one opportunity to present Christ to a crowd of people, how would you get their attention? To what need or value would you appeal?

3. The mime figure in the drama reminds us that Christ is not bought but celebrated! How fares the celebration of Christ in your church? What moods do you sense during the Lord's Supper?

"What Do You Mean, 'He's Here Already' ?"

A Chancel Drama for Lent 6 (Series C)

Bible Text:
Luke 19:28-40

Focus:

Jesus comes in ways unexpected. His is not the way of proud glory and strutting honors. He chooses instead the quiet path of humility and service.

Characters:

KINGMAKER—front-man for the president of the United States; hurried; bossy; in control
KELLY—subservient secretary
PRESIDENT—a voice on the phone heard only by Kingmaker

Setting:
An office.

(*As the scene opens,* KINGMAKER *sits at his desk which is covered with papers. He speaks on the telephone.* KELLY *stands in waiting at his desk.*)

KINGMAKER: (*Reads from paper on desk as he listens; pauses for response.*) Yes, sir. As far as I know, the hotel is cleared through security. ETA is set for 4:00 p.m. at the airport. We'll follow Route B for travel to the downtown convention center. (*Pause for response.*) No, sir. The president has not talked to me on that. Can you hold a second? (*Puts caller on hold; and turns to* KELLY.) Kelly, any word on flight plan?

KELLY: Air Force One has not called yet, sir. We expect a call within the hour.

KINGMAKER: (*Back to caller.*) No word yet on that, sir. We expect confirmation from Air Force One by 0900 hours. (*Pause for response; condescendingly.*) Nine o'clock! (*Covers phone; to* KELLY.) Where did they get these guys in the White House? No military background at all. (*Pauses a few moments.*) We'll call you immediately. (*Pause.*) Right. (*Hangs up phone; back to* KELLY.) Got your list? Let's run down it one more time. Color guard?

KELLY: Check, Chief.

KINGMAKER: Band?

KELLY: Check, Chief.

KINGMAKER: Room service?

KELLY: Check, Chief.

KINGMAKER: Chuck the "Check, Chief," will you, Kelly? (*Thinks a moment.*) Buses for demonstrators?

KELLY: Six Greyhounds will leave the demonstrators off three blocks away. They'll walk to the hotel with the signs.

KINGMAKER: What did we settle on for signs?

KELLY: "We love you, Mr. P," "Run again, Mr. President," "Four more years!"

KINGMAKER: Scratch that one, Kelly, right now.

KELLY: Check, Chief.

KINGMAKER: (*Looks up in frustration at* KELLY.) Babies?

KELLY: Excuse me?

KINGMAKER: I said, "Babies." Will there be any babies in the crowd?

KELLY: I suppose.

KINGMAKER: What do you mean, "I suppose"? Get me babies.

KELLY: How do I do that?

KINGMAKER: Call your relatives. I don't know. But I want young families with babies in the picture. Got it?

KELLY: Check, ah-h-h, Mr. Kingmaker.

KINGMAKER: Get on it, right now. (KELLY *exits.* KINGMAKER *dials phone; pauses for ring.*) Bill? Kingmaker here. It's go for Route B from the airport. (*Pause for response.*) Right. (*Hangs up phone; shuffles paper; phone rings again.*) Kingmaker. (*Pauses for response; sits up in chair as he discovers who it is.*) Yes, Mr. President. (*Pause.*) She's fine, thank you. (*Pause.*) We're ready to go here, Sir. We've got a welcome planned that will set the town on its ear. Good media stuff. Great cooperation from the locals, too. (*Pauses and takes on shocked look.*) Oh. I see. Yesterday already. (*Pauses again.*) You

did? (*Pauses.*) Yes, Mr. President. (*Pause.*) Oh,
that's O.K. We'll call everyone concerned.
(*Pause.*) Good-bye, Sir. (*Sits in wonder; calls
for* KELLY.)

KELLY: (*Enters.*) Yes, sir.

KINGMAKER: You won't believe this, Kelly.

KELLY: What?

KINGMAKER: It's off.

KELLY: It's off?

KINGMAKER: He's here already.

KELLY: What do you mean, "He's here already!"?

KINGMAKER: The president drove down in his son's
VW.

KELLY: You're kidding. No one saw him, did they?

KINGMAKER: Just a few friends who met him at the
hotel.

KELLY: But the demonstration . . . the limo . . .
the welcome . . . the band!

KINGMAKER: He's here already. (*In disbelief.*) He arrived yesterday. In a VW. Ditched the Secret Service and all. (*In stream of consciousness.*) What
a risk! And tonight Maggie and I are supposed
to have supper with him. That's what he said.
I heard him. Imagine it. The president showing
up in town like that. I've seen everything now.
Not military at all. (*Pauses to think.*) Not at all.
Not safe. Not smart. (*Reconsiders.*) But, Kelly,
tonight Maggie and I will have supper with the
president. And you should have heard how
kindly he made his invitation. (*Thinks again.*)

He may lack class, but the man has heart. (*Both*
KINGMAKER *and* KELLY *freeze, then exit.*)

Primers for Preaching

1. Jesus may reveal himself in ways and at times
totally unexpected.

2. While on earth, Jesus chose service over glory,
humility over honor, and oneness with humanity
over power. How different would our world be if we
who bear Christ's name also lived as he lived?

3. "Who would have ever thought. . .?" is a
phrase that can prefix one event after another in
the life of Christ, especially during Passion Week.

4. We build our neat, little God-systems, anticipating our Lord's every move, only to find that God
comes at will and in the way God chooses.

Discussion Starters

1. Kingmaker in the drama was so caught up
with arrangements and details that he lost touch
with the fact that the president was a person. How
do schedules, programs, and plans sometimes sti-
fle the Christian's relationship with Christ?

2. Which do you think is emphasized more in
the church today: the theology of glory emphasizing honor, success, and power, or the theology of
the cross emphasizing humility, service, and sacrifice?

3. Where in the church have you seen "king-
makers" at work? That is, where have you seen
people who think of Christ only as glorious King
rather than as Suffering Servant as well?

4. How can the church emulate the Suffering
Servant? Where will people be surprised to find us
in ministry?

Dramas from an Upper Room

Six Dramas
Based on the Upper Room Discourses of Jesus
in John

"Jesus Saves"

A Chancel Drama for Ash Wednesday

Bible Text:

John 13:31—14:14

Focus:

God's plan of salvation is all tied up with Jesus Christ. Jesus saves. Some people want more. Some want less. Some want something different. This, however, is the plan, and it is the message of the church.

Characters:

HANK—impartial; a leader
CLAIRE—impatient; sarcastic; critical
WILL—timid; uncertain
JOANN—business-like
LARRY—has biting sense of humor
BOB—Gamaliel revisited; patient; discerning

Setting:

A simple "outdoor" setting. A homemade sign reading "Jesus Saves."

(*As the scene opens, six members of the Board of Church Properties meet outside Grace Church to discuss the mysterious appearance of the sign. Characters should wear coats or jackets to give the impression of being outdoors.*)

HANK: Well, there it is. (*Points to sign.*)

CLAIRE: We've seen the sign, Hank. It's been up since a week ago Sunday.

WILL: Are you sure we need to meet outside for this, Hank? It's a bit nippy tonight.

HANK: We'll go in after we get a good look at the situation.

JOANN: I just wish we knew who put up the sign. Was it a member?

CLAIRE: No, it wasn't a member. No member of our church would put up a sign like this. It's the work of vandals if you ask me, ecclesiastical vandals, with an obvious lack of artistic taste. Let's take down this eyesore before anyone else gets a look at it.

WILL: Hold on just a minute here. Take that sign down, and you may be sending a message to the community you'll regret.

CLAIRE: What message, Will?

WILL: The whole neighborhood knows it's here. They've seen it for 10 days now. Take down the sign and they might think we don't believe it.

CLAIRE: Believe what?

WILL: Believe what the sign says, Claire, that "Jesus saves."

CLAIRE: Oh, Will, you can be such a nerd sometimes. Of course we believe what the sign says. That's not the point. It's an eyesore. That's the point.

JOANN: In my opinion, both the artistic quality and the message of the sign warrant rapid removal.

WILL: The message of the sign? Now JoAnn, be careful. There is nothing at all wrong with this sign's message.

JOANN: Nothing wrong with it if you want to insult passersby.

LARRY: This sign insults passersby? Now I've heard everything.

JOANN: To say that Jesus saves is to say that people need saving.

LARRY: The woman's a theologian.

JOANN: And to say that people need saving is to say that they're unable to handle their own destiny, that they're dependent. They may even be made to feel that they're sinners.

LARRY: Oh, no, wouldn't that be terrible.

JOANN: In my opinion, people don't want to be told that they're in need of saving anymore. They want to be told that they're doing just fine, and that they can do even better.

LARRY: Maybe we should put up a different sign, one that reads: "You can do it!" I can't believe this!

JoAnn: As a matter of fact, that's not a bad idea. "You can do it!" I like it, Larry. I like it. It'll build membership. That's for sure. People don't want to feel bad about themselves.

Larry: Fine. And we could hold "You can do it!" seminars and sell "You can do it" buttons. I'll ask pastor if he'll write a book titled, "You can do it!" and we can sell it on TV and radio.

JoAnn: You go ahead and make fun, Larry. You're out of touch with the church of the future, though, I'll tell you that.

Hank: Bob, you've been very quiet. What do you think about the sign?

Bob: I think we could leave it up for a little while and see what happens. Maybe something good will come of it. Maybe not. Let's try and find out who put it up and why.

Claire: Catering to vandals now, are you, Bob?

Bob: No, I just wouldn't want to hurt anyone's feelings. After all, they didn't exactly paint an obscenity on the sign, did they?

Claire: Bob, you're always too patient. You always want to wait. Why, if you had your way, this church would have never been built. You'd still be waiting for the construction costs to come down. Hank, I'm telling you, let's get the sign down and go home.

Larry: No one has asked my opinion on the sign yet.

JoAnn: That's right, Larry, we haven't.

Larry: I'll tell you what I think. I think the sign is incomplete. It doesn't say enough.

JoAnn: O.K., I'll bite. What more should it say?

Larry: Well, as it stands now, it could be taken to mean that Jesus saves everyone. It doesn't say who Jesus saves. We should be specific.

Claire: It doesn't say *whom* Jesus saves, Larry.

Larry: Whose idea was it, anyway, to have women on the Church Properties Board?

Hank: So, Larry, how would you change the sign, if you could?

Larry: I'd leave the "Jesus Saves." Only underneath it, I'd put the name of our church, Grace Church.

Claire: Don't you think that's a bit parochial, Larry? People will think we're saying that Jesus only saves Grace Church.

Larry: JoAnn here wants to increase membership. Let's give this approach a try. Exclusiveness. It works with private clubs and country clubs. It will motivate people to join us.

Claire: It's been tried, Larry. Remember the Pharisees?

Larry: Sure beats "You can do it!" if you ask me.

Will: What about it, Hank? Can we head inside?

Hank: Are there any other comments before we go inside? (*No response.*) Fine. Then let's just settle this matter around the table in the board room. (*All begin to exit.*)

Claire: As far as I'm concerned, the matter is settled. The sign comes down. After all, we have an image to maintain.

JoAnn: What will people think?

WILL: I don't know, we've tipped our hand now, so to speak. We may have to leave it up.

LARRY: (*Puts arm around* BOB.) Come on, Bob, let's find some paint.

CLAIRE: Touch that sign, Larry, and you'll have me to contend with. (*All exit.*)

Primers for Preaching

1. It's amazing how we Christians can sometimes make life in Christ so difficult for ourselves.

2. In John 14:6, Jesus calls himself "the way, the truth, and the life." In that simple statement, he claims exclusive rights to his role as the world's Savior and Lord.

3. Not everyone is comfortable with grace. Grace says forgiveness is a gift. Some people would rather earn forgiveness.

4. Strange, how good news can sound like bad news! The church tells people that they need to be saved and can be in Jesus Christ. Then people get upset because they don't like anyone telling them that they're in trouble.

Discussion Starters

1. What causes people in the church to argue over a truth as simple as "Jesus Saves"?

2. The name of the church in the drama is Grace Church. How do the characters reveal that they have a hard time with the notion of grace?

3. How sensitive must the church be to the world's reception of its message? Can we ever be over-sensitive?

4. What words would you choose to summarize the Christian faith?

"Pardon Me, but Who Died?"

A Chancel Drama for the Second Wednesday in Lent

Bible Text:

John 14:15-31

Focus:

Some people live as if God had died. They find no reason for hope. Sometimes churches even reflect this despair. The church is meant to offer people hope through Christ and his Spirit.

Characters:

The three mourning characters (Numbers 2-4) maintain a mood of detached sadness throughout the drama. The whistler (Number 1) is enthusiastic and bubbly throughout with an honest spirit of curiosity.

Setting:

A room with seats for at least three.

(*As the scene opens, a happy, whistling visitor [Number 1] comes upon three people dressed in black and obviously in a mourning mood. He must decide to join them or whistle on. The three should sit on chairs and assume positions of despair.*)

1: (*Enters whistling.*)

2: We'll have to ask you not to whistle.

1: Oh?

3: Please, do not whistle.

1: It's a habit. Sorry.

4: We are not comfortable with whistling.

1: I said I was sorry. It's a habit. It just happens. You know. I don't even think about it.

4: We do not know. Think about it from now on.

1: A friend of mine says he can't believe how I can whistle all the time. He says I'm one of the happiest people he knows. Says I make him feel good every time I come around.

4: And what did you say?

1: Why, I said, "thank you." That's what I said.

4: We will not be comfortable with you.

3: That is for certain.

1: Well, pardon me, but who died?

4: What do you mean, who died?

1: You look like a funeral in 3-D.

3: You should probably move on.

2: You should move on. You won't be happy here.

1: You're right there. That's for sure. (*Silence.*) You three don't really make a person feel welcome.

4: We are not comfortable with you.

1: I could try a few jokes, you know, to cheer you up. Laughter's good medicine. Why just last week I picked up an article on laughter and it said. . . .

4: We are not comfortable with you.

1: Just what does make you comfortable?

3: We are uncomfortable most of the time.

1: I bet you don't smile much either. Say, what if we play that game where I try and get each of you to smile. If you smile you're out. Last left not smiling wins. O.K.

2: Good-bye.

1: (*Silence.*) So. . .what do you do here?

3: We mourn mostly.

2: We are *the* mourners. As I said, good-bye.

1: You are *the* mourners, huh?

4: We come together to mourn.

1: Then someone has died!

4: Death is always with us.

1: Certainly looks that way.

2: The world is very evil.

3: Getting worse all the time.

4: It is not good.

1: And so you mourn?

4: That is what we do.

1: The three of you.

2: There are more. Don't be deceived. Our number is great. We happen to be on duty tonight.

1: Some duty.

3: It is an honest reaction to the way things are.

1: I suppose someone has to do it.

4: Everyone should, if they have any moral integrity, that is.

2: There is no more honest an enterprise. All the rest is cover-up, nothing more than make-believe camouflage.

1: I think I'm getting depressed.

2: Follow your instincts. (*1 goes off and sits alone.*)

3: At least we are not alone.

2: You are alone, but we are not.

4: We have each other. We are a fellowship, so to speak.

2: Our number will grow. You'll see.

1: Misery loves company! Is that it?

2: Our number will grow.

1: (*Stand.*) There is reason for hope!

2: Camouflage!

3: (*Chuckles.*) There is no reason for hope.

1: You sound so certain, so sure of yourself.

2: That is why we are here, to say that there is no reason for hope.

1: Hope is dead?

2: Death is always with us.

1: Then God has died?

3: You said that. We didn't. God is silent. That's for certain.

1: But do you believe God has died?

4: There is no greater reason to mourn in all the world than that one.

1: But do you believe that God is dead?

4: God is silent. He may be dead. Some believe he is dead.

1: (*Sits again; silence.*) How long will you do this?

2: Do what?

1: Mourn.

2: As long as it takes.

1: As long as it takes for what?

2: For people to know how tragic it is. For everyone to see the truth.

1: The truth?

2: That we are left alone, and that is very sad.

4: You may join us, you know.

2: But you must not whistle.

3: No music at all is allowed.

4: Will you join us?

1: I don't think so.

4: You hesitate. You may join us.

1: I still have reason to hope.

2: There is no reason to hope.

3: Death is always with us.

1: I'll be leaving now.

2: Please, do leave.

4: Leave us . . . for now.

1: I'll exit whistling.

3: If you respected our wishes, you would not whistle.

1: I do not respect hopelessness.

2: Well spoken, but sadly misdirected. Leave us to our mourning. Good-bye.

1: (*Begins to exit Stage R.*) I am leaving.

4: Just where are you going?

3: You're going to try and find God, aren't you. You think you'll find him, don't you?

2: You will be disappointed.

1: I do not need to search for God.

2: Face it. You will end up dressed in black just as we are.

1: I'll exit now, whistling. I want the people watching us to hear me exit, whistling.

4: What people?

2: There are no people watching us.

1: (*Points to audience.*) You don't see them.

3: (*Shades eyes; looks out in direction of audience.*) We see no one.

2: (*Shades eyes.*) No one at all.

1: You are alone after all. Your mourning has left you blind.

4: That is your opinion.

1: You cannot see beyond your sadness, can you?

2: You had better leave now.

1: Blindness can be healed. (*Pauses.*) I'll exit now, whistling. I want them to hear me whistling. (*Exits whistling.*)

4: He left us.

3: He left whistling. He whistled for them, wherever they are.

2: They are not. He's gone, but he'll be back. Won't he? Well, won't he?
(2,3, *and* 4 *assume freeze positions; lights out; exit.*)

Primers for Preaching

1. Death is a powerful force in our lives. We are afraid of it. We run from it. We deny it. Yet we must never give it the last word.

2. Jesus promised that he would never leave us desolate or orphaned (John 14:18). Still, there will

be times when we feel desperately alone and forsaken. Faith, in such times, whistles in the darkness, trusting that, evidence to the contrary, our Lord is still here.

3. The church is meant to offer people hope in the face of despair and the music of the gospel in the silence of death.

4. If people who are orphaned by society do not find hope in the church, where will they find it?

Discussion Starters

1. What traits of the whistler in the drama are clearly characteristic of Christians at work in the world?

2. Recall a time when it seemed that God was absent from your life. How did you meet God again?

3. "Laughter's good medicine," says the whistler. Do you agree?

4. Who are your "whistlers," bringing hope and the presence of Christ to your down times?

5. In John 14:27, Jesus promises a peace which the world cannot give. How does the whistler in this drama characterize that peace?

The Sedentary Life

A Chancel Drama for the Third Wednesday in Lent

Bible Text:

John 15:1-17

Focus:

The Christian life is a productive life given to service and love. Yet many Christians still approach life only as consumers, those who take and receive but do not give.

Characters:

SID—haughty; self-focused; detached; confident; dressed in a clownish way, wearing bright colors, a bold tie, and a mix of plaids, checks, and stripes

STORYTELLER—tells story without notes; enthusiastic; tells story as one would tell it to a child

NUMBERS 1 - 7—people in waiting; resemble line of servants waiting to meet the whim of nobility

Setting:

A room with one tall stool.

(*As the scene opens, seven people stand in row stage left of a man sitting on a tall stool.*)

SID: (*Sits center stage.*) Sedentary: an adjective; 1. characterized by or requiring a sitting posture: a sedentary occupation;

1-7: (*Unison.*) 2. accustomed to sit much or take little exercise; 3. abiding in one place; not migratory; referring to animals that move about but little or are permanently attached.

SID: I beg your pardon!

STORYTELLER: Once there was a man who lived the sedentary life. He lived away from everyone on purpose and kept on hand just enough people to serve his every need and fancy. He always sat. No one who knew him said he did anything but sit and expect others to serve him. He was quite comfortable, striking it rich on the stock market as he did. There were, of course, the expected pains attendant to the sedentary life, particularly in one place, but the man never complained. The benefits far outweighed the costs. For instance, when the man became hungry, he simply said:

SID: I am ready to eat. Bring me my dinner.

1: (*Brings sandwich and glass of milk on tray.*) Your dinner, Sir. (*Waits as* SID *eats.*)

STORYTELLER: And there it was, at his beck and call, the food of his choice to be devoured in a sitting position, of course. He had no idea where the food came from or how it was prepared. He simply called for it and it was there.

SID: Take it away.

1: Yes, Sir. (1 *takes tray; exits off stage; returns to place.*)

STORYTELLER: And so it continued day by day and year by year.

SID: The news. I am ready to hear the news. Bring me the news.

2: (*In reporter fashion.*) Hunger continues to plague much of Africa. If help does not arrive soon, many will die. . . . Locally, a boy injured last evening in a traffic accident died this morning at Mercy Hospital. The driver of the car that struck him has been charged with driving under the influence. In sports . . . .

SID: That will be enough. Too much bad news. I need to be entertained. Bring me entertainment. (2 *returns to line.*)

3: (*Approaches* SID; *plays guitar or another instrument.*)

SID: Boring. I'm bored.

3: Would you like to hear an Iowa joke? I do Iowa jokes.

STORYTELLER: And so he was entertained.

SID: I am ready to be read to. I want to hear someone read.

4: (*Approaches* SID.) I shall read some poetry to you, Sir.

SID: Fine. Poetry. That will be fine.

4: I never knew a night so black
   light failed to follow in its track.
   I never knew a storm so gray
   it failed to have its clearing day.
   I never knew such bleak despair
   that there was not a rift somewhere.
   I never knew an hour so drear
   love could not fill it full of cheer.*

SID: Well done, well done. Yes, love. A wonderful thing, to be loved. (*Pause.*) I am ready to make a decision. I need advice. Bring me advice. And bring me something to decide.

5: (*Approaches* SID.) The room needs painting, Sir. What color shall it be painted?

SID: Ah, color schemes. I know something about that. Let's see. (*Thinks.*) What do you think?

5: Purple is a fitting color, I would say.

SID: Purple, you think? (*Pause.*) Then purple it is! (5 *returns to line.*)

STORYTELLER: Time passed, and the man grew older. (STORYTELLER *walks over to* SID *and puts a gray beard on him, powdering his hair to make him look older.*)

SID: I'm getting cold. I'm ready for my coat. Bring me my coat.

6: (*Approaches* SID) Here is your coat, Sir. It will keep you warm. (*Helps him on with coat.*)

SID: Seems colder than usual this year.

6: Yes, Sir. (*Returns to place.*)

---

*John Kendrick Bangs

SID: I'm ready for a friend. I need a friend. Bring me friendship.

7: (*Approaches* SID) I will be your friend.

SID: Good. I need a friend. Sit here with me.

7: How long would you like me to sit here with you? (*Sits down on floor.*)

SID: As long as I need you. It may be a while.

7: Fine.

SID: You are my friend?

7: You pay me to be your friend. I guess that makes me your friend.

STORYTELLER: And there the two sat for many hours at a time.

SID: I'm grateful for your friendship.

7: I'm grateful for your salary.

SID: You may take a break.

7: With pay?

SID: Yes, of course, since we are friends.

STORYTELLER: The old man sat and called for service as he needed it, but less and less as time went on. Finally, the days grew colder. (6 *brings him coat.*) The old man wore his coat almost always and shivered all the same. Then one day, the servants at his beck and call heard him say:

SID: I'm ready now to die. Bring me to heaven.

STORYTELLER: Those lined up to serve him wondered what to do. No arrangements had been made. For the first time, no one in the line was able to respond.

SID: I said, I'm ready now to die. Bring me to heaven.

STORYTELLER: There came to him not a soul.

SID: I'm ready now. I'm ready to go to heaven.

STORYTELLER: He summoned God as if God were in his line of servants.

SID: If there is a God somewhere, you can come and bring me to heaven. I'm ready now.

STORYTELLER: (SID *drops head in death posture.*) And when the old man died, the servants, I'm told, took care of all the arrangements. (*Pause.*) Now those who've heard this story say there's a lesson to be learned here. The life that takes and never gives is the most tragic life of all. We're most like God when we give, and so when we give, we'll be the most fulfilled. The sedentary life is not the life of love; it is the life of consumption. . . and one that ends not well.

(*All exit.*)

Primers for Preaching

1. Jesus said, "By this my Father is glorified, that you bear much fruit, and so prove to be my disciples" (John 15:8). The test of our discipleship is not that we're consuming grace and receiving mercy but that we're putting grace to work in service.

2. Too many lives today are lived from a consumer's perspective. We approach life on the basis of what we get. Even our religion is approached from this perspective. Those who abide in Christ have discovered that real living is serving, not being served.

Discussion Starters

1. Talk about consumerism in the church today. Where are there signs of Christians defining the faith and the church in terms of what they get rather than in terms of what they give?

2. The Storyteller in the drama says, "We're most like God when we give, and so when we give, we'll be the most fulfilled." That's image of God theology, noting how we'll always find fulfillment and satisfaction when we reflect God's nature. What can Christians do to brighten their reflection of God's image? Or in Jesus' terms, what can we do to remain in him? (John 15:4)

3. Which is easier for you: to give love or to receive love?

4. Try and answer this question: What does God give the person who has everything? (In other words, what is the plight of the person whose entire life seems complete *without serving others?*)

In the Middle of "In-between"

A Chancel Drama for the Fourth Wednesday in Lent

Bible Text:

John 15:18—16:11

Focus:

The Bible speaks often of the struggles Christians face. One such struggle is the tug-of-war taking place within the Christian between the world and the Spirit. Both ask for loyalty. Both ask for commitments. Those who try to satisfy both at the same time, however, ask for much and receive little.

Characters:

NUMBERS 1, 2, and 3—representatives of the world, promising earth-bound success

NUMBER 4—A Christian form between world and Spirit

NUMBERS 5 and 6—representatives of the Spirit, re-
lentlessly pursuing the Christian to make choice

Setting:

A small bridge divides the two opposing factions
(optional).

*(As the scene opens, Number 4 stands between
three representatives of the world and two representatives of the Spirit, each side pulling at his
or her allegiance.)*

1: You!

4: Me?

1: Yes, You!

4: What can I do for you?

1: Hah! What can you do for us? You must be kidding! It's what we can do for you!

2: We've been watching you there for some time.
How long have you been out there?

4: For some time.

2: How long do you plan on staying out there?

4: I'm not sure. I haven't decided.

2: We can help you decide. You can't live halfway,
you know.

1: You need to commit yourself, to be loyal.

4: Perhaps.

3: Your time is limited. You're wasting it out there.

4: What do you have to offer?

1: What do you need?

4: Success. I need success.

2: We have that.

4: I worry about having enough money.

3: We have that, too.

4: I need some freedom, some independence.

2: Come with us and you will be truly independent.

1: How about some power over your own destiny?

3: And how about some good friends?

2: Good times?

1: An award here and there, a commendation.

3: We have credentials for you.

4: I have some of that now.

3: But it isn't what you live for, is it?

2: It isn't what you love, is it?

4: I haven't decided yet.

1: You'll never get it all unless you go for it.

2: Whole hog.

3: Wide open.

1: Full throttle.

3: No holding back.

1: Now you're talking!

5: Be careful.

6: Beware.

5: Watch yourself.

6: You're easy, aren't you?

4: And what do you mean by that?

6: You feel the pull from their side, don't you?

4: Maybe I do.

6: You've been up at night worrying about it, haven't you?

4: No, I haven't.

5: Be careful. Go with them, and you'll lose.

6: You're losing now already.

4: I am not losing. I am trying to decide.

5: You are not winning out there.

4: I haven't decided. That's all.

5: You don't have forever.

4: They told me the same thing.

5: Well?

4: I need time.

6: There is much for you here with us.

4: They offer much as well.

6: But can you trust them?

4: I'm not even sure I can trust myself.

6: Do you trust us?

4: I suppose I should.

6: You should?

4: I should be able to trust people who speak for God.

6: You should, but will you?

4: I haven't decided. I'm afraid.

5: Afraid of what?

4: I might miss something. . . from their side, I mean.

5: Join them and you may miss more than you think.

2: Join them and you won't have any fun.

1: You'll look foolish sometimes.

3: You'll have to excuse yourself from certain situations.

2: People will whisper concerning your self-righteousness.

4: Look, we're in this together, aren't we? I mean, it's all God's good, green earth. We're all human, aren't we? Can't we approach this with some humanity?

5: What do you want?

4: I want to enjoy both—the material and the spiritual.

5: That is a possibility. You can enjoy both.

4: Well, then, I'll stay here.

5: No, you cannot stay there. You are in the middle of in-between. You are nowhere. You have made no commitment. Where is your heart?

4: This is God's world. They are a creation of his as well.

3: We are? Oh, yes, certainly. We are.

2: Sure we are.

5: Where is your heart? You don't have much time.

6: Not to decide is to decide.

4: Give me a break.

5: There are no breaks. We'll keep coming after you.

2: As will we. There are no breaks. Every minute counts.

5: There are no breaks. You must decide.

4: And then I will be at peace?

5: It depends on what you decide. Is it peace you want?

4: It's peace I want.

5: Then seek what makes for peace. Decide.

4: I will. . . soon.

(*Freeze; then all exit.*)

Primers for Preaching

1. For the Christian, the world is both blessing and curse. On the one hand, the world is God's creation, redeemed by Christ. It is the arena of witness and in itself witnesses to the Creator Lord. On the other hand, the world lures the Christian away from life in the Spirit, tempting to sin and asking for loyalty.

2. Whom will you serve? The world with its promises of success, wealth, and commendation? Or the Spirit, calling you to service and to inner peace.

3. Those who try to live in both the realm of the world and the realm of the Spirit lose out in both

cases. They settle for receiving only a part of what each offers.

4. The life of Christ—and his realistic warnings—show clearly that to be a Christian asks much of us. For every Christian there is a cost attendant to following Christ.

5. A difficult question: Does our at-ease comfort with the Christian faith signal that we've compromised our loyalties?

Discussion Starters

1. Talk about the secularization of the church. Where has the church given in to the world and compromised its role as prophet and conscience?

2. Where do society's and the church's demands on the Christian come into conflict? Identify the battlegrounds.

3. Describe a time when you were caught "in the middle of in-between." What did you decide and why?

Losing It

A Chancel Drama for the Fifth Wednesday in Lent

Bible Text:

John 16:12-33

Focus:

The great, glad victory of Jesus Christ, a victory shared by every Christian can be obscured by the bad news we encounter. The crescendo of bad news builds until we hear no victory shout from Christ.

Characters:

STORYTELLER—a teacher-type; a storyteller with a lesson to teach

TED—begins exhuberant and ends deflated; a seeker

BILL—only gives if he gets

SUE—too busy to share joy; will do what's necessary, nothing more

SAM—a balloon-buster

AMY—sarcastic; cutting

LOU—somewhat baffled by Ted's mood

Setting:

The chancel area can serve as the office setting.

(*As the scene opens five people are stationed around the chancel area in different locations.*)

STORYTELLER: (*Enters.*) It is said that erosion, even death, can happen quite unexpectedly. Take, for instance, a science experiment. A frog is put in a beaker partially filled with water. The beaker is placed over a very slow flame. Gradually, ever so slowly, the water rises in temperature. The frog, quite pleased being a frog in a beaker of water, never notices that things are heating up. Degree by degree the temperature rises, and the frog notices nothing until at last, the frog dies, a victim unawares. Erosion happens gradually. That which we have is taken out from under us, before we even know it. Take, for instance, Ted. Ted woke this morning to a day of good news such as he had never known before. Listen. He'll tell you.

TED: In one morning, mind you! What a day! I'm a father, a new father with a healthy daughter. That's one! Then I get a call. I'm promoted, he says. I didn't even know they were considering me! Can you believe it! Vice President! That's two! Then, get this, then I get a call from the loan officer and she says that our home loan application has been approved. A new home. That's three! Family! Job! Home! All in one day. I'll tell you, there's not a man more blessed on the face of the earth. Well, what do you think? Well? Isn't that something? (*No response.*) I just can't believe it!

STORYTELLER: I'm sure you share Ted's joy. He was flying on the wings of victory. I'll tell you, he wore it on his face. It was unmistakable. Ted was a winner. Not unlike the way Christians feel inside, some would say, when their spirits soar and they feel a part of the winning glory of Jesus Christ. Now what do you do when you're on top of the world? Sure, you share it with a friend. Right?

TED: (*Walks over to* BILL.) Bill, you won't believe it! (*Beams.*) You're looking at the most fortunate man alive.

BILL: I'm sure, Ted, there are people more fortunate than you. You could be a bit more modest.

TED: I'm a father, Bill. We had a daughter this morning!

BILL: Congratulations.

TED: And I've been promoted!

BILL: Congratulations.

TED: And our home loan was approved.

BILL: Congratulations.

TED: That's it? Congratulations. You don't sound too excited, Bill.

BILL: I'm happy for you, Ted.

TED: Don't I get a hug or something?

BILL: Don't I get a cigar or something?

TED: Oops, forgot the cigars.

BILL: Bring a cigar, and I'll give you a hug.

STORYTELLER: Not exactly a festival . . . what Ted got from Bill, but then Bill wasn't much in the mood, or so it seemed.

TED: (*Walks over to* SUE.) Sue, it's my day of days! Mary and I were blessed with a baby girl this morning. (*No response.*)

TED: Well?

SUE: That's great, Bill! Give me the hospital and room number and I'll send Mary flowers.

TED: Fairview Hospital, room 324, Sue.

SUE: Fine, Bill, see you later.

TED: But Sue, besides the baby, we . . .

SUE: I'll catch you later, Ted. Have to run.

STORYTELLER: Degree by degree, you see, the joy is whittled down. What Sue's problem was, one can't be sure. Maybe she was preoccupied. Or maybe she wished she was in the hospital with a baby in her arms herself. Good news can breed jealousy, you know.

TED: (*Walks over to* SAM.) Sam, ready yourself. (*Beams.*)

SAM: I heard all about it already, Ted. It's old news. Bill called. Beat you to the punch. Thrice blessed, huh?

TED: That's right.

SAM: And no cigars. Funny guy, that Bill.

TED: So what do you think, Sam?

SAM: I think you're not quite yourself, Ted. You never look quite this way on other days.

TED: Well, Sam, this isn't just another day!

SAM: In fact, Ted, you can be something of a frump sometimes.

TED: What's that supposed to mean?

SAM: Take it for what it's worth. I am happy for you, Ted. Now, if you don't mind. I need to run.

TED: Sure, Sam. (*Walks away.*) A frump, he said. Imagine that.

TED: (*Walks over to* AMY.) Amy, Amy, Amy!

AMY: Ted, Ted, Ted.

TED: Amy!

AMY: Ted, why are you wearing that dumb tie again? If I've told you once, I've told you twice, you look like a twit in that tie. It's too wide and it doesn't match a thing.

TED: Amy, I have to tell you . . .

AMY: Look, Ted, change ties, and I'll talk with you. O.K.?

TED: Come on, Amy, I've got news, news, news!

AMY: And I'm sick of that tie.

TED: Well, listen, Amy, just forget it, alright? Frankly, I'm not too crazy about your dress either. Anyway, you're not my wife.

AMY: I've said more than one *Te Deum* for that.

TED: What's a *Te Deum*?

AMY: Oh, Ted, you can really be a loser sometimes.

STORYTELLER: And now the water is brought to a boil, and the frog dies unawares.

TED: (*Walking by* LOU) Say, Lou.

LOU: Hey, how's it goin', Ted?

TED: Do you really want to know, Lou? Do you?

LOU: Well, it's sort of a colloquialism, you know. "How's it goin'?"

TED: You don't really want to know, do you, Lou?

LOU: Sure, Ted. Sure I do. How was your day?

TED: Lou, my day was a loser.

LOU: Yeah, I've had days like that.

TED: A loser, I tell you.

LOU: Anything special happen?

TED: No, Lou, nothing at all.

STORYTELLER: Now take this as a parable on the good news that you have. You're blest of all the human race to claim a share in the victory of Christ. But careful, there. Good news gets old and muffled out by bad news all too easily. Erosion of the spirit can catch you unawares.

(*All exit.*)

Primers for Preaching

1. The drama is a parable on having good news and finding oneself deflated and silenced. Though Jesus has overcome the world (John 16:33), the world may still overcome us if we are not careful. The world is not always ready to be cheered.

2. Erosion of the spirit is a gradual thing. Joy is lost not suddenly but degree by degree.

3. From whom do you take your mood cues? From those around you or from deep inside where the Spirit of Christ dwells?

4. Which wins out more often for you: bad news or good news?

5. Like the birth of a child (John 16:21) our new life in Christ is powerful enough to silence every pain and sorrow.

Discussion Starters

1. How is one's enthusiasm for the gospel drained today? How does erosion happen in the Christian life?

2. What makes it so hard for us to be affirming, positive-minded people?

3. Paraphrase what these words of Jesus mean for you, personally: ". . . be of good cheer, I have overcome the world" (John 16:33). What specifically do you hope to overcome through the power of Christ within you?

4. If you were to share the "good news" with someone today, what items would be on your good news list? Which of these items are secure and abiding, yours for keeps? Which are temporal and tenuous?

Six People, One Pew

A Chancel Drama for the Sixth Wednesday in Lent

Bible Text:

John 17

Focus:

What if six people who share the same pew in the same church could tell you something about themselves? You might get a lesson in diversity and in unity. There is a miracle that happens every time people share a pew and worship together. This little drama seeks to manifest the miracle.

Characters:

LORNA—older woman (60 or older)
BRAD—teenager
DON—man (30-45 years old)
MOLLY—child (6-9 years old)
BARB—woman (30-45 years old)
JACK—young man (21-25 years old; minority, if possible)

Setting:

Church pew facing the congregation.

(*As the scene opens, the six characters share a church pew.*)

Introduction   (*May be read by Worship Leader.*)
Every time you come for worship, you find your place and share a pew with another believer in Christ. It's a miracle that you and that person and all the others who worship from that pew can do it together. Jesus prayed for that miracle. Despite all our differences he prayed that we'd be one—in worship and in service. Now I wonder what it would be like if we could pick a pew and listen to the people who share it speak of their experience. I think we'd see the miracle of fellowship in the church made possible by the gospel.

LORNA: Yes, Sir. I've sat in this pew for over 50 years, and my parents sat here before me.

BRAD: (*To* DON.) Dad, do we have to sit here every Sunday? The lady down at the end there (LORNA) grinds her teeth.

MOLLY: (*To* BARB.) Mom, is the service almost over?

BARB: Molly, the service hasn't started yet.

LORNA: Children should be seated in the rear of the church, if you ask me.

DON: This is our church pew.

LORNA: We're only a few.

MOLLY: But we sit here each Sunday.

JACK: And hear what's true.

BARB: This is our church pew.

BRAD: We're only a few.

LORNA: We sit here together

MOLLY: And hear the good news!

LORNA: I like formality.

BRAD: Formality's a bore!

MOLLY: What's formality?

DON: Game's on today. Wish I knew the score.

JACK: I'm a Republican.

LORNA: No place for politics, the church. (*Whispers.*) I'm a Republican, too.

DON: Good for you.

BRAD: I haven't decided yet.

DON: You'll be a Republican, son.

BARB: I'm a Democrat.

DON: You are?

BARB: I guess I never told you that.

DON: A Democrat!

MOLLY: I'm a Christian. Does that make me a Republican or a Democrat?

JACK: I believe in free will. I chose this church.

LORNA: I believe in predestination. I was destined to come here.

JACK: I chose this pew.

LORNA: I inherited this pew.

MOLLY: There are a lot of older people in this church.

LORNA: The children should worship from a pew in the rear.

BRAD: There's the preacher. I don't like to sing.

BARB: Oh, wonderful, a hymn, just the thing!

JACK: Nice fella, the pastor.

BRAD: Not much of an athlete.

LORNA: No one can top Pastor Beckenwalter. No one.

MOLLY: Mom, have we come to the part yet where he talks so much?

BARB: Soon, Molly. Here, rest your head on my lap.

DON: Have room for another? Time for my nap.

BARB: Don, shame on you. People can hear you. Shame on you.

LORNA: Did you hear that? Did you hear that? (*Pause.*) I like the old ways.

BRAD: I like the new.

JACK: Whatever the pastor says.

LORNA: He's too new. And this is my pew.

BRAD: Just once I'd like to sit on the end of the pew.

BARB: Hush, now, listen.

MOLLY: What's he talking about?

DON: I disagree.

JACK: Oh, sure, I see.

LORNA: I don't see. I don't see at all. Old Pastor Beckenwalter sure stood tall.

(*Usher may enter and pass collection plate down.*)

DON: I give what I can.

JACK: I give what I can.

LORNA: I give a tithe. Wish the young people tried.

MOLLY: Mommy, can I have a quarter?

BARB: A nickel will do.

MOLLY: But I want a quarter.

BRAD: Good. We're almost through.

(*Usher exits.*)

DON: Pray for the people, some sick and some blue.

BARB: Pray for the people who sit in this pew.

MOLLY: Mom, get my coat. I'm ready to go.

DON: I drive a truck.

JACK: I'm in med school.

LORNA: I'm retired.

BRAD: Hey! So am I!

BARB: I'm a homemaker.

MOLLY: I think I'm a Democrat.

JACK: Not much in common, you and I.

LORNA: Agreed. I'm different from you five.

DON: For me Christ died.

LORNA: For me Christ died.

BARB: For me Christ died.

BRAD: For me Christ died.

JACK: For me Christ died.

MOLLY: For *us* Christ died.

JACK: And the Lord will bless us,

BARB: And keep us.

BRAD: The Lord will make his face shine on us

LORNA: And be gracious to us.

DON: The Lord will look upon us with favor. . . .

LORNA: Oh, I wish they hadn't changed the wording of that.

JACK: Lorna!

MOLLY: And the Lord will give us peace. Now, Mom, is it time?

DON: This is our church pew.

LORNA: We're only a few.

MOLLY: But we sit here each Sunday

JACK: And hear what's true.

BARB: This is our church pew.

BRAD: We're only a few.

LORNA: We sit here together.

MOLLY: And hear the good news.

BARB: Now, Molly. Now.

(*Six gather belongings and exit.*)

Primers for Preaching

1. Despite all of our differences in the church, we are one in Christ. The gospel makes us one. For all of us Christ died.

2. Christian fellowship is a miracle to be celebrated.

3. Diversity in the Christian church broadens the church's perspective and enhances the scope of the church's witness.

4. Christ's high priestly prayer for unity among his people (John 17) is fulfilled with every worship service in our congregation.

Discussion Starters

1. Church growth experts emphasize the need for homogeneity in a church as a significant factor in encouraging growth. In other words, the more the membership is the same, the more the membership will grow. Do you agree?

2. What changes in your church have left you cold? Has a change ever left you feeling on the outside of your church fellowship?

3. How do you feel about the practice in some churches of having the children in Sunday school during the worship service? Is it important for a worshiping community to have children present?

4. When have you seen political differences affect the unity of a Christian parish? What political issues today enter into the church's conversation and witness because they are ethical issues as well?

5. What can a Christian parish do to enhance both its diversity and its unity and so fulfill the prayer of Christ in John 17?

Were You There?

A Dramatic Worship Event for Good Friday

Setting:

The lights in the church should be dim except when reading by the congregation is necessary. The sanctuary proper should be dark.

The Reading of the Holy Gospel for Good Friday

(*Stand*)

PASTOR: In the Name of the Father, and of the Son, and of the Holy Spirit.

CONGREGATION: Amen.

PASTOR: Beloved in the Lord. On this night we commemorate with solemn thanksgiving the sufferings of our Savior on the cross, his death, and his burial. Listen to the Gospel of the Lord written in the Gospel according to St. John, chapter 19, verses 17-42.

(*The Pastor reads the Gospel. He or she may choose to read the lesson from the midst of the people or from the rear of the church. The reading of the Holy Gospel completed, the congregation is seated.*)

The Chancel Drama
"Were You There?"

WOMEN'S VOICES (*3 Women*):
Surely he has borne our griefs
and carried our sorrows;
yet we esteemed him stricken,
smitten by God, and afflicted.
But he was wounded for our transgressions,
he was bruised for our iniquities;
upon him was the chastisement that made
us whole,
and with his stripes we are healed.
All we like sheep have gone astray;
we have turned every one to his own way;
and the Lord has laid on him the iniquity
of us all.
(Isaiah 53:4-6)

JESUS' VOICE: Daughters of Jerusalem, do not weep for me, but weep for yourselves and for your children. (Luke 23:28)

SOLO VOICE (*sings*):
Were you there when they crucified my Lord?
Were you there when they crucified my Lord?
Oh, sometimes it causes me to tremble,
tremble, tremble.
Were you there when they crucified my Lord?

(6 figures have been standing in the chancel since the beginning of the service, heads bowed. They should either be vested or dressed in black and white. They raise their heads when the hymn verse has ended.)

1: I was there. I wept as he walked his way to death.

2: Tears are death's companion.

3: I watched a man die once. He was old and sick. His days had been full. Still I cried for him.

4: When my father died, I wept alone. I did not want anyone to see me.

1: We wept openly. It was our custom. We wept for all, for others who would not weep. Death called for tears.

4: You knew him?

1: Jerusalem knew him. And he knew us, perhaps better than we knew ourselves.

4: I was there. I carried his cross.

5: You there! Take the prisoner's cross!

4: I was enlisted, you understand.

6: Who were you, Simon, to bear the Savior's cross?

4: And tell, me, who are you to wear a cross around your neck, and place it on your steeples, and sign it on your children's breasts?

3: We are people of the cross.

4: I did not see you on the hill that day.

3: We were there, I tell you. We were there.

2: It was duty drawn and duty done. I nailed him to the cross (*The sound of hammer against nail is heard.*)

5: Make ready the cross! Steady now. He is your charge.

1: Hammer and nail. Hammer and nail. I can hear it still.

2: I nailed him to the cross. (*The sound of hammer and nail stops.*)

5: Now raise the cross. Go easy with him. (*Pause.*) There.

CHOIR (*sings*):
Were you there when they nailed him
   to the tree?
Were you there when they nailed him
   to the tree?
Oh, sometimes it causes me to tremble,
   tremble, tremble,
Were you there when they nailed him
   to the tree?

3: I was there. I heard him pray.

(*A single bell tone may sound.*)

JESUS' VOICE: Father, forgive them for they know not what they do.

2: We thought it arrogant. It was enough to see the sign above his head, "Jesus, the King of the Jews." We cast lots for his robe.

5: Take a chance.

4: Life is a game of chance.

2: Gamble it. Risk it.

1: See if fate be on your side.

2: Oh, why not? Count me in. One will win. Why not me?

(Two bell tones may sound.)

JESUS' VOICE: Today you will be with me in paradise.

1: I was there. I was a thief.

2: How unlike us.

3: Hardly the kind one would expect to see in paradise.

4: The man's only a thief.

5: Who is he to promise paradise? Who is he?

3: "This is Jesus, the King of the Jews."

6: How unlike us, this criminal.

3: Hardly the kind one would expect to see in church.

4: Hardly the type one would like to see in our church.

5: He promised him paradise!

3: I was there. The Master looked at me. And spoke:

(Three bell tones may sound.)

JESUS' VOICE: Son, behold your mother.

6: Ever the servant. Ever the gentle one.

5: His mother should not have come. This is no place for her.

2: This is no place for anyone sensitive to his suffering.

4: Why are we here?

1: Why *have* we come?

6: We are always here.

1: Always?

6: Ever since the first, we are always here.

5: His mother should not have come.

(*Four bell tones may sound.*)

Jesus' Voice (*with a shout*):   My God, My God, why hast thou forsaken me?

6: I was there in the silence.

4: I have been alone in the silence as he.

1: Where is God when one dies before his time?

2: I looked for God, and I did not find him.

5: There is no answer. (*Silence.*)

3: Some say there is no God.

5: Oh, there is a God.

3: Then where is he now? Where is God now? (*Silence.*)

2: He'll be gone soon. The day is passing.

5: The sky is darkening.

(*Five bell tones may sound.*)

JESUS' VOICE: I thirst.

5: Give the man vinegar.

4: Give the man clothing.

3: Visit him.

1: And give him food.

2: Quench the man's thirst.

6: Ever since the first, we are always here.

(*Six bell tones may sound.*)

JESUS VOICE: It is finished!

2: Sir, it is the end.

5: Hush.

3: In Bethlehem, fair city, a Savior Christ is born.

1: And he astounded the teachers of the temple.

3: Peter, follow me. Andrew, follow me. You sons of thunder, follow me.

4: Bring the children here. Of such is the kingdom of God.

6: There was a man who had two sons.

4: Ephphatha! Be opened!

3: And he went away by himself to pray.

1: The good shepherd lays down his life for the sheep.

2: Sir, it is the end.

4: He loved them all.

6: He loved us all.

2: Sir, it is the end.

5: I know.

2: He said that it is finished.

5: I heard him.

6: Ever since the first, we are always here.

1: And like a son falling asleep in his father's arms, he cried aloud:

JESUS' VOICE: Father, into your hands I commit my spirit!

1: And having said this, he breathed his last.

(*Seven bell tones may sound.*)

5: Truly this man was the Son of God!

SOLO VOICE (*sings*):
　　Were you there when they laid him in the tomb?
　　Were you there when they laid him in the tomb?
　　Oh, sometimes it causes me to tremble,
　　　　tremble, tremble.
　　Were you there when they laid him in the tomb?

1: The stone is very heavy.

2: We will roll it in place together.

3: We are finished here.

1: The stone is very heavy.

2: What will happen now?

3: We will roll the stone in place and go home.

2: Home? I had forgotten about home. Our home has been with him.

1: We must roll the stone in place now. All together now, push!

2: It's done.

1: We leave him here, our Master. It is a great stone that seals this tomb.

2: The women will come the morning after Sabbath.

1: Yes, the morning of the first day.

(*Reprise of seven bell tones.*)

4: O God in death's dark night,

5: Send us the morning.

4: We watch and wait, on the ramparts of the night.

5: Joy will come in the morning when once this Sabbath has passed.

6: Ever since the first, we are always here.

Small Group (*Organ plays softly while small group sings.*)
Were you there when God raised him
   from the tomb?
Were you there when God raised him
   from the tomb?
Oh, sometimes it causes me to tremble,
   tremble, tremble.
Were you there when God raised him
   from the tomb?

The Confession

PASTOR: Look on us, Lord. We come in repentance.

CONGREGATION: We must die to sin if we are to live.

PASTOR: Let us confess our sins.

CONGREGATION: We confess, Father, that we have made ourselves the focus of life. We care more about ourselves than about others. We make decisions and act with self-interest as our primary motive. Put to death in us this sinful pride. Our Savior sacrificed all for us. He took our sins upon himself. He carried the full weight of our trespasses. O Father, for the sake of his perfect sacrifice, forgive us.

PASTOR: The cross is at the center of our worship. We remember this day the lengths to which Christ went to do the Father's bidding. His fellowship with the Father brought him to Calvary. May you be so at one with the Father that you, too, will pick up your cross and follow in the Savior's way of sacrifice. You are forgiven through Jesus Christ. Now bear the fruits worthy of your repentance.

CONGREGATION: Amen.

Hymn

"My Song Is Love Unknown"

Sermon

Offerings

The Bidding Prayer

The Solemn Recessional

(*In token of our Savior's death, the Processional Cross is carried out of the sanctuary. As the Recessional stops at each of three stations, the pastor and the congregation speak the Scriptural versicles.*)

At the first station:

PASTOR: He was wounded for our transgressions. He was bruised for our iniquities.

CONGREGATION: Upon him was the chastisement that made us whole, and with his stripes we are healed.

At the second station:

PASTOR: Far be it from me to glory

CONGREGATION: Except in the cross of our Lord Jesus Christ.

At the Third station:

PASTOR: Greater love has no man than this,

CONGREGATION: That a man lay down his life for his friends.

Hymn

   "Now the Light Has Gone Away"
   Stanzas 4-5